Do You Have A Million Dollar Idea?

Do You Have A Million Dollar Idea?

✦

Learn the Seven Steps of the Invention Process Through One Man's Incredible Journey!

Marty J. Carty

iUniverse, Inc.
New York Lincoln Shanghai

Do You Have A Million Dollar Idea?
Learn the Seven Steps of the Invention Process Through One Man's Incredible Journey!

iUniverse books may be ordered through booksellers or by contacting:

iUniverse
2021 Pine Lake Road, Suite 100
Lincoln, NE 68512
www.iuniverse.com
1-800-Authors (1-800-288-4677)

The views expressed in this work are solely those of the author and do not necessarily reflect the views of the publisher, and the publisher hereby disclaims any responsibility for them.

Photo credit is given to Hughes Photography Studio in Marion, Ohio.

ISBN: 978-0-595-44474-8 (pbk)
ISBN: 978-0-595-88801-6 (ebk)

Printed in the United States of America

To my wife, Patricia, and our four wonderful children: Shaun, Amanda, Elizabeth, and Kristen.

Life is complicated enough, with plenty of risky turns in our daily lives. We need our families to stand by us as we venture into new territory. The patience and support from my family was crucial as we went through this incredible invention and book writing journey together.

Contents

Acknowledgments

I would like to thank the following people for their tireless efforts and priceless contributions to the writing of this book:

- Rusty Fischer

  - Rusty was the perfect fit as my co-writer. Not knowing what to expect as I undertook the process of writing my first book, I leaned on Rusty, and he came through brilliantly.

- The SealPak Innovations Team

  - James Brooks, Dinah Jessie, and Jeremy Simpkins. They gave me feedback on my early writings and encouraged me to continue on by expressing their feeling that many people will benefit from reading the ShurTrax story.

  - ShurTrax investors. If not for your monetary assistance, ShurTrax would still be only a dream.

- ShurTrax Customers

  - You have made everyone's efforts worthwhile.

Thanks again to all of you!

Perhaps you've been mulling over a passion, idea, or invention for years, but you're just not there yet. This book may serve as the incentive you need to rip away the negative baggage that has been clinging to you, holding you back, and preventing you from pursuing your idea.

I say just go for it! After all, it is the American dream, isn't it?

Whatever your reasons for taking the trip—be they personal or professional, inspiration or motivation—be prepared for a journey that will rival the most amazing roller coaster ride you have ever been on.

The following story is my story, and I hope it helps you plan, execute, and realize your dream. Remember, there may have been over three hundred thousand patents issued last year, but there's always room for one more!

Next year, why not make it yours?

Preface

✦

Have a Million-Dollar Idea? Get in Line!

Great ideas need landing gears as well as wings.

—Adolph Augustus Berle

So you think you have an idea that could make millions. Or, maybe you don't have an idea yet but are sure that a world-changing product is soon to emerge from your creative mind. You want to know how to take that idea and turn it into a viable product.

Well, join the crowd. According to the Web site of the United States Patent and Trademark Office (http://www.uspto. gov/), "Patent examiners completed 332,000 patent applications in 2006, the largest number ever." Furthermore, "USPTO trademark examining attorneys took final action on 378,111 trademark applications, a 36 percent increase over the previous year."

In this fast-paced world of information and technology, new products are entering the marketplace at breakneck speed.

Don't believe me? Then you've obviously never had insomnia! Simply watch TV from just after midnight to just before dawn and you'll witness the best—and worst—that the inventors of this country have to offer.

From fold-up colanders that "stack up or slide away" to tabletop vacuum cleaners shaped like cones, and from exercise machines that resemble spaceships to nose-hair clippers that double as corkscrews and flashlights, there has never been a better time to bring your invention to market.

But buyer—and inventor—beware. There has never been a better time to get ripped off on your way to market. Merely Google the keywords "patent your invention" and you'll be the lucky recipient of some 2.5 million sites, all eager to "help" you through the complicated and intricate patent-pending process.

Some of these companies can legitimately help you; most of them cannot.

According to the American Patent and Trademark Law Center, "Beware of services of companies who offer to 'review,' 'market' or 'submit your invention to manufacturers.' There are many such firms who prey on small inventors and tell them their invention is 'the best thing since sliced bread'. Some companies may insist on an expensive and immediate patent. Others may tell you that you don't need a patent, and for a fee (usually in the thousands of dollars) they will 'market' your invention to thousands of firms. Once they have three to ten thousand dollars of your money, you will be hard-pressed to even contact them."

My name is Marty J. Carty, the inventor of a patented product known as the ShurTrax System—a safer alternative to add traction weight to your vehicle. After experiencing the invention process for myself, I decided to write a book called *Do You Have a Million-Dollar Idea?*

Several people have stopped me to ask, "How did you do it? How did you come up with a product that is now being sold in auto parts stores all over the country? How did you go from brainstorm to reality by starting your own company?"

My answer is always the same: "How long have you got?"

Seriously, though, the journey from inspiration to running your own company is neither a short nor an easy one. Once upon a time an inventor needed only to spend a few thousand hours in his/her basement, emerge with a newfangled product that flipped eggs or filled tires, and the money came rolling in. But such days have long since "lost their patent," as we say in the industry.

Today there are vultures perched atop every outlet for idea shoppers, be it online or off—all of them eager to come in and scavenge the latest brainstorm, invention, or scheme. Unwary inventors are more likely to lose their shirts paying unscrupulous companies to help them patent their idea than they are to ever see a dime of their invention's profits—that is, if the invention ever gets to market in the first place.

This book is based on my own personal story of taking an idea and bringing a new product into reality. It took time, money, energy, blood, sweat, tears, and jeers, but by trusting my gut and learning the ropes, I was able to bridge the gap between idea and reality and live to tell the tale!

Along the way I learned what I call the *Seven Steps of the Invention Process*, which I will share with you on the pages of this book. These steps are:

- **Step #1:** *Discover a Problem*

- **Step #2:** *Know When to Spend and When to Do It Yourself*

- **Step #3:** *Leave Your Excuses Behind*

- **Step #4:** *Understand Patents and Prototypes*

- **Step #5:** *Raise Capital*

- **Step #6:** *Establish a Pipeline*

- **Step #7:** *Enjoy the Pull-Through*

My hopes are that by reading this book, you will learn the seven lessons that will save you time, energy, and expense when you embark on the journey for yourself. Remember, every journey needs a road map. Use these seven steps as the rest stops along your journey, and take comfort in knowing that I've gone through the trial and error for you.

Now all you need to do is reap the benefit—and enjoy the ride!

Perhaps you've been mulling over a passion, idea, or invention for years, but you're just not there yet. This book may serve as the incentive you need to rip away the negative baggage that has been clinging to you, holding you back, and preventing you from pursuing your idea.

I say just go for it! After all, it *is* the American dream, isn't it?

Whatever your reasons for taking the trip—be they personal or professional, inspiration or motivation—be prepared for a journey that will rival the most amazing roller coaster ride you have ever been on.

The following story is my story, and I hope it helps you plan, execute, and realize your dream. Remember, there may have been over three hundred thousand patents issued last year, but there's always room for one more!

Next year, why not make it yours?

Marty J. Carty

Million-Dollar Memo:

There's never been a better time to bring your invention to market. But buyer—and inventor—beware. There has also never been a better time to get ripped off on your way to market

---

The Seven Steps of the Invention Process

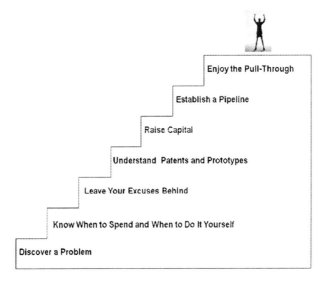

- Enjoy the Pull-Through
- Establish a Pipeline
- Raise Capital
- Understand Patents and Prototypes
- Leave Your Excuses Behind
- Know When to Spend and When to Do It Yourself
- Discover a Problem

Step #1

✦

Discover a Problem

Most people spend more time and energy going around problems than in trying to solve them.

—Henry Ford

All of our lives, we've been taught to think of problems as bad things. "Houston, we have a problem" calls to mind not an opportunity to bring space travel to a new level, but the catastrophe that almost befell those Apollo 13 astronauts. If you've got a million-dollar idea, that's not a problem—that's a solution! This is a chapter about discovery: of beginning your own voyage to the unexplored, just like those Apollo 13 astronauts.

Maybe you haven't started your journey yet; maybe you're contemplating some ideas that are just that so far—ideas. You could be witnessing a problem in the making and an opportunity on the rise. How to find out?

Take the test with this P-R-O-B-L-E-M Solver, to see if your idea:

- **P-rovides an answer to a question:** Questions answered are problems solved. That is why we should always be on the lookout for problems that can be turned into solutions.

- **R-ectifies a situation:** Maybe your coffee won't stay warm in the morning. Maybe your soda won't stay cold. Inventions should solve problems.

- **O-pportunity in the making:** Start looking at problems as opportunities—that's what they are!

- **B-reaks the rules:** "Idea people" are rule breakers at heart. We look at a rule and see how it can be bent, if not broken entirely. Typically these are the rules of science and commerce, and some of the best ideas in history have come from breaking the rules.

- **L-eaves others smiling:** When you solve a problem, you don't just do it for yourself; you do it for hundreds, thousands, and even hundreds of thousands of people. Now, doesn't that make you want to be a problem solver?

- **E-nters new territory:** Don't be afraid to imagine a problem that lives outside of your comfort zone. Instead of seeing a problem but ignoring it because it's too far out of your range, research and find mentors to help you on your way.

- **M-akes life easier:** Will your idea make someone's life easier? This is often a problem waiting to be solved—and a million-dollar idea in the making.

After reading this chapter, I hope you see problems in a whole new light—as opportunities rather than obstacles and as assets rather than liabilities. In our business, inventing new products or services to fill a need, problems aren't the end, they're just the beginning!

Million-Dollar Memo:

If you've got a million-dollar idea, that's not a problem—that's a solution!

The "Yeah, But ..." Test

Some ideas pop with a bang, not a whimper. Mine started with a gobble. It was Thanksgiving weekend 2002 when I began my own journey toward my million-dollar idea. Of course, most inventors are idea people; they see ideas everywhere, often when and where others aren't quite looking. I was no exception. I had contemplated several ideas in the past, but just never felt that any of them were worth pursuing—until now.

I realized that if I were to put forth the efforts required to make something like this go, my idea would have to pass the "yeah, but ..." test. How does your idea stack up? Ask yourself, using the "yeah, but ..." test:

- **Idea:** I figured out how to keep coffee warm all day.

- **Yeah, but** how will people plug it in on the go?

- **Idea:** I just designed a hooded sweatshirt that stays closed with Velcro.

- **Yeah, but** will the kids still buy it?

- **Idea:** I just created the most fantastic flavor of ice cream *ever!*

- **Yeah, but** how much will it cost to get it made?

You get the idea. In many ways, the "yeah, but ..." syndrome is a problem in itself—meaning, of course, that it's an opportunity waiting to be discovered. When we are our own devil's advocate, we often solve the "yeah, but ..." syndrome long before we get too far down the wrong road.

Fortunately, I had plenty of experience playing devil's advocate—and not just to myself. In one of my previous jobs, I spent most of my time teaching and training associates on lean manufacturing techniques. Lean manufacturing is a management philosophy focusing on reduction of waste to improve overall customer value. During these training sessions I was always prepared for the skeptical associates who would say, "Yeah, this sounds all right on the surface, but what about …" This taught me to be ready and able to answer this simple question when it came to my own product ideas. I decided that if I couldn't work out all of the possible "yeah, but …" questions on my own, then I would push the idea to the side and hope another one would soon come along.

Million-Dollar Memo:

Most inventors are idea people; they see ideas everywhere, often when and where others aren't quite looking. I was no exception.

Giving Thanks
(For a Problem)

Ideas are like true cravings: you may not know what you're in the mood for at first, but you know it when you see it—and were my eyes ever open. In fact, I was in luck! A problem that led to an idea which seemed like a "keeper" came to me on Sunday morning of Thanksgiving weekend 2002.

The winter of 2002–03 came quickly for us in central Ohio. By Thanksgiving weekend, we had a couple of significant snowfalls. Although nothing close to keeping the kids out of school, enough snow fell to make the roads slick and parking lots aggravating—problems made worse when I would drive my full-size Dodge Ram 1500. Don't get me wrong, I loved my truck. It just didn't have enough weight in the rear. This problem is not only limited to Dodge Rams, but can be found in any pickup truck or rear-wheel-drive car.

In previous years, I had placed concrete blocks or sandbags in the back of my truck in an attempt to solve the problem, or accepted "spinning around" by using nothing at all. I had heard horror stories about accidents leaving passengers paralyzed or killed when a concrete block or frozen sandbag would fly through the rear window like a missile. This is not to mention the shifting and rolling around hassles of these types of objects. All this caused me to accept the slipping and sliding from my rear wheels, and I didn't use any additional weight for a few years.

It was Sunday morning of Thanksgiving weekend when I jumped into my pickup and headed to church. Pulling into the slanted parking lot, I felt nervousness setting in when I looked over the lightly snow-covered area and wondered if I would be able to get enough traction to drive out later. After church was over, I jumped back into my truck and began to slowly pull out of the parking lot.

Then, just as I feared, my truck began sliding. I knew I couldn't continue going forward so I tried backing up. Uh oh! This was not working either. Matter of fact, this was worse! I was sliding backward and could not stop. I was going to slide right into another car when thankfully the truck stopped just short of a fender bender.

I rolled down my window to look back at my dilemma when I heard a voice call down from the heavens (okay, or maybe just the church parking lot), "Hey, do you want me to pull your Dodge out with my Chevy?"

I couldn't believe it! There stood a friend of mine who was also leaving church. We always shared a little ribbing with each other on the whole Dodge vs. Chevy issue. How embarrassing! There'd be no winning any arguments with him for awhile!

I held my breath, hit the accelerator, and slowly began to slip, slide, and move forward. I'm glad no one walked in front of me because I was moving now and not going to stop for anyone or anything.

As I pulled out onto the road, my tires grabbed the surface, and I was headed for home, but not without wondering what I was going to do about adding weight to my truck this winter. After all, this was only November and I was not about to put up with this all winter. I thought there must be something out there available to buy by now that would help me out.

I decided I would begin looking into it Monday morning.

Million-Dollar Memo:

Ideas are like true cravings: you may not know what you're in the mood for at first, but you know it when you see it.

Poka Yoke Philosophy
(It's No Joke)

I arrived at work on Monday morning and asked around to find out if any of my co-workers knew of anything out there that I could purchase to solve my slipping and sliding problem. It actually came as no surprise to me when no one knew of anything other than cinder blocks or bags filled with sand or salt.

Already my mind was spinning. Could this be a problem that no one had solved yet? Could I come up with something to solve it first? It was an idea man's dream—and the first stirring of an inventor's blood.

I got onto the Internet and did a quick search to see if I could find an answer to my dilemma. Nothing could be found, so I began to rethink my strategy. Why should I want to purchase an inferior product like sandbags? Why couldn't I design a product of my own? After all, one of the techniques I taught associates at work was called "poka yoke." *Poka yoke* is a Japanese phrase that means "to mistake-proof a process."

Mistake-proofing was a big part of my business philosophy. Over the years, I had trained others not to get mad or accept poor quality in products or in their job assignments but to use the mistake-proofing process to help them determine if a new solution to their problem was the best answer. Once you find the root cause of the problem, the idea is to put something in place to fix the problem or prevent future errors from occurring.

Keeping that philosophy in mind, I quickly decided it was time to practice what I had been teaching. The root cause of my dilemma was that pickup trucks are inherently too light in the rear end, causing the rear tires to slip and slide in inclement weather. The current solution was to throw junk into the back of your truck to add weight. I knew there had to be a better way. Now I just had to think of a system or product that would accomplish the task of easily, cleanly, and safely adding and removing weight to my pickup truck as needed.

Million-Dollar Memo:

Could this be a problem that no one had solved yet? Could I come up with something to solve it first? It was an idea man's dream—and the first stirring of an inventor's blood.

Problems Lead to Questions; Questions Lead to Answers

My thoughts for the product quickly turned to a water-filled container and led to plenty of questions. I realized I had found a possible solution; now I needed to know if it would pass the "yeah, but ..." test.

The first "yeah, but ..." that came to mind was "yeah, but what would happen when the water froze?" I figured there must be a plastic or vinyl type of material available that could withstand freezing and expanding water.

Most people have been conditioned to believe that water expands twice its volume when it freezes. This isn't true. Water does expand, but not nearly as much as some have been led to believe. I also wondered about some more integral questions:

- How could I keep the water from sloshing from side to side?

- How much does water weigh?

- How many gallons would be required to meet the needed weight?

- How could I make a one-size-fits-all product?

  Other types of questions quickly followed, such as:

- Will people actually buy something like this?

- What size is the market?

- Can I get it made at a price people are willing to pay?

- Will it actually help my truck in slick conditions?

- What should I call it?

- How much money would it take to get this manufactured and marketed?

- Will the time and effort required pay off?

- Should I do this myself or pay an invention company to do it for me?

- Should I get this patented?

- How do you patent something and how much does it cost?

- If I tell my friends and co-workers about this, am I vulnerable to someone stealing my idea and making millions from it?

- How much am I willing to lose if the idea doesn't work?

I listed them that way, even though I know it's hard to take them in all at once, but these are exactly the types of questions you should be prepared to answer when you take your own "yeah, but ..." test. Remember: problems lead to opportunities, and questions lead to solutions!

This led to two of the most important questions I had to ask myself: "When do I spend money, and when do I do it myself?" and "Do I have what it takes?"

Million-Dollar Memo:

I realized I had found a possible solution; now I needed to know if it would pass the "yeah, but ..." test.

Step #2

✦

Know When to Spend and When to Do It Yourself

The big shots are only the little shots who keep shooting.

—Christopher Morley

When would-be inventors discover a problem to solve, they are faced with a choice: invent the solution themselves, or outsource the nuts and bolts to something known as an "invention company."

Obviously, bringing your invention to market is a daunting task. I admit I was very intimidated at first, but in the end I chose to work on my project myself and not hire an invention company.

After all, who else would put their heart into this with as much enthusiasm as I would? I also was afraid of being duped into forking over my hard-earned money to people I didn't know. What if they scammed me through some loophole in the contract and stole my idea or, just as bad, did nothing with it due to a lack of effort? I knew that effort was one thing I could give this project more of than anyone else.

Before I made that decision, though, I wanted to give these "invention companies" their fair shake. Maybe I didn't know best; maybe someone could help me. What I discovered wound up falling under the "three strikes" category: two strikes for them, one strike for me!

Million-Dollar Memo:

When would-be inventors discover a problem to solve, they are faced with a choice: invent the solution themselves, or outsource the nuts and bolts to something known as an "invention company."

Strike One:
The Personal Visit

Before deciding to take my invention to market alone, I initially contacted two different "invention help" companies I found on the Internet. It just so happened that the first one had a home office close to me in Columbus, Ohio, so I paid them a visit.

Their proposal went something like this: "We would love the opportunity to take your idea to market." Then they explained what they would do for me. Basically, they would do a drawing of the product, conduct a market search, file for a patent, and take the idea to trade shows in hopes of finding an existing manufacturer who would buy the idea and pay me royalties.

Sounds pretty tempting, right? I'll admit that the idea of passing the burden on to someone else seemed appealing—at first. After all, they made it sound so easy. Market search and patent filing and trade shows—it was the inventor's equivalent of supersizing your supersize!

Then I stepped back to consider the reality of what they were offering. Let's say this company brought my product to market, handled all the paperwork, red tape, and bureaucracy of filing the patent, and it got picked up at a trade show. Well, if a company were to actually get interested in my idea, the maximum going royalty for the inventor is 5 percent. Not so bad when we're talking millions in potential profits, but was I really willing to give away that much of MY idea? I understood the costs for manufacturing and advertising and connections in the marketplace, but 5 percent? To my way of thinking, *I* should have gotten the 95 percent, not them.

Then there were the fees the invention company wanted: the cost was approximately $9,000 for their services. I was skeptical of giving someone nearly ten grand to do work that I could—and should—do for myself.

Although they would have filed a patent for me, I later learned that I could have an attorney do the same thing for less than half that amount: $4,000. They also promised to provide a 3-D drawing on CAD software that could be rotated to show potential manufacturers the product idea. Big whoop! I eventually got an actual prototype for $500—by doing it myself.

Sitting in this guy's office, I could see how they might persuade so many people to give them $9,000 and all their ideas. They're the experts, right? Before jumping in with both feet—and nine thousand great reasons to regret my decision in the morning—I decided to do some research on them and discovered they were involved in lawsuits from several clients. These particular lawsuits were attributed to this company filling their clients' heads with "you can't miss with this idea" thoughts.

This certainly caused me to back off from doing business with them. However, people sometimes get what they deserve. What do I mean by that? Well, have you ever watched *American Idol*? Some people want to believe in their idea (or talent) so much that they set themselves up to be scammed (or severely disappointed). It's worse than being star struck; it's like getting sucker punched by your dreams.

Take this invention help company, for instance—and the people who pony up that kind of dough for the chance at making their dreams come true. If the invention company told these inventors their idea was no good, they would probably just go somewhere else with their invention. If they discovered that nobody ever made money by giving this company $9,000, they may say, "Well that's because the other ideas weren't as good as mine." Do you see my point? They almost scream out, "I want to believe in this dream so much I will fall for anything!"

A wise man once said, "If you don't stand for something, you'll fall for anything." If strike one had me standing on my own two feet, wanting to take my future into my own hands, then strike two had me running for the door!

Million-Dollar Memo:

It's worse than being star struck; it's like getting sucker punched by your dreams.

Strike Two:
An "Invention House" is Not a Home

The second company I checked out was called something like "Invention Home"—we'll call them "strike two". I sent them my idea and they promised to do a patent search. Thanks to my research, I expected the search to be certified by their attorney and asked them up front to have that done.

After two months, I received the results from their search. To say I was disappointed was putting it mildly. Not only was it *not* signed by an attorney (as I'd specifically requested), but it was very impersonal and simply stated, "it is our professional opinion that you should be able to obtain patent protection on your idea."

They didn't even say *what* was patentable.

This much I already knew for myself: patents are always issued with claims of exactly what was patented. For example, the ShurTrax patent ended up with 10 claims, with the most important being the flexibility of the vinyl material. So for my purposes, their two-month evaluation was "patently" worthless.

I immediately wrote them and asked for clarification—and an attorney signature. Six hours later, I received a letter from their Vice President of Marketing advising me they were "no longer interested in continuing any work for me" and that they "wished me luck."

They *did* refund my money, and I had a patent attorney conduct another search. That same attorney who conducted my search did such a great job that I kept him on as my patent attorney throughout the completion of the patent process.

So much for strike two....

Million-Dollar Memo:

Patents are always issued with claims of exactly *what was patented.*

Strike Three:
Time for Me!

Eventually, after careful consideration and the "two strikes" from above, I decided to dig into this project myself.

I've often looked back on my decision to tackle my problem myself, wondering what type of success I might have had—or missed out on—if only I'd let an invention company handle the grunt work for me. Would my success have come sooner? Would it have come without all the trials and tribulations to follow? Or, perhaps, did those trials and tribulations in some way help create my success?

What's that line by Robert Frost? "Two roads diverged in a wood, and I—/I took the one less traveled by,/And that has made all the difference" ("The Road Not Taken"). I believe I would not be telling you this story in quite the same way if I'd handed my idea off to someone else and let them run with the ball.

Would my life have been easier? Sure; absolutely. But no one ever said success was easy, and now when I go to sleep at night I rest easy knowing that I own my success—bought and paid for. Whatever happens, success or failure, the ultimate responsibility rests with me.

What about you?

Million-Dollar Memo:

Two roads diverged in a wood, and I—/I took the one less traveled by,/And that has made all the difference.

—Robert Frost

Tips for Getting Help

I don't want to color your decision about doing it yourself or hiring an invention company to help you through the process. This book isn't about me so much as it is about *you*; I want you to learn from my story, and then apply those principles to your own journey. If you do decide to work with an invention company, the Federal Trade Commission (FTC) has some good advice to follow on their Web site (http://www.ftc.gov/):

- The American Inventors Protection Act of 1999 gives you certain rights when dealing with invention promoters. Before an invention promoter can enter into a contract with you, it must disclose the following information about its business practices during the past five years:

  - How many inventions it has evaluated;

  - How many of those inventions got positive or negative evaluations;

  - Its total number of customers;

  - How many of those customers received a net profit from the promoter's services; and

  - How many of those customers have licensed their inventions due to the promoter's services.

- This information can help you determine how selective the promoter has been in deciding which inventions it promotes and how successful the promoter has been.

- Many fraudulent invention promotion firms offer inventors two services in a two-step process. One involves a research report or market evaluation of your idea that can cost you hundreds of dollars. The other involves patenting or marketing and licensing services, which can cost you several thousand dollars. Early in your discussion with a promotion firm, ask for the total cost of its services, from the "research" about your invention through the marketing and licensing. Walk away if the salesperson hesitates to answer.

• Many fraudulent companies offer to provide invention assistance or marketing services in exchange for advance fees that can range from $5,000 to $10,000. Some even offer to finance the full amount to entice inventors into making a quick decision. Reputable licensing agents rarely rely on large up-front fees.

• Unscrupulous invention promotion firms tell all inventors that their ideas are among the relative few that have market potential. The truth is that most ideas don't make any money.

Million-Dollar Memo:

*This book isn't about me so much as it is about **you**; I want you to learn from my story, and then apply those principles to your own journey.*

Step #3

✦

Leave Your Excuses Behind

Our greatest weakness lies in giving up. The most certain way to succeed is always to try just one more time.

—Thomas A. Edison

If you have an idea that is just waiting to be developed, you need to ask yourself a very basic question: do you have what it takes? What I mean is, "Do you have the confidence required to see your idea through?"

It may seem like a simple question, but most people you know probably don't have what it takes to stay the course. And it really is a course—an obstacle course—with potholes and dips and bumps and speed traps and plenty of hecklers lining your path, just waiting for you to stumble so they can take your idea and carry it across the finish line or bullishly watch you fail.

Races are not just won by the fleet of foot, but also the firm of mind. The course may have obstacles, but with ingenuity and determination you can get around, over, under, or straight through anything you put your mind to.

It may take awhile—it may seem like it takes forever—but just keep putting one foot in front of the other and you will complete the "idea obstacle course" and make it to your final destination: success.

Million-Dollar Memo:

Races are not just won by the fleet of foot, but also the firm of mind.

No More Excuses!

In business, the saying goes, "Time is a deal killer."

In the invention business, the saying goes, "Excuses are idea killers."

When we make excuses, we rob ourselves of the tools necessary to succeed. The path to success is hard enough when you're firing on all cylinders. Every excuse you make damages your performance and makes the journey that much more difficult. If confidence is the air in your tires, then excuses are the potholes that leave you with four flats—and no spare—on your journey to invention.

Many people have great ideas but do very little with them. Why? Because they don't have the confidence, know-how, and/ or attitude required. Forget about all the other excuses they may use. The fact is, that's exactly all they are—excuses. I have heard them all since I began this journey. They go something like this: "Can you believe it? I once had a great idea and someone later made a million dollars off the same idea...."

Inevitably, I ask why they didn't do anything with the idea, and then I stand back, count to five (though it usually doesn't take that long), and listen as the excuses begin to flow. You may have heard—or even used—these very same excuses yourself.

They go something like this:

- "I was too busy."
- "I didn't know how to go about it."
- "I didn't have the money."
- "I'm too old."
- "I'm not smart enough."

- "I couldn't get anyone to help me."
- "I have kids to take care of."
- "Blah, blah, blah ..."

I have news for you: I was all of those things, too. I have even better news for you: leadership, confidence, and attitude are not birthrights. People are not born possessing a monopoly on these characteristics. When we were newborn babies, we all needed adults to take care of us and nurture us until we were old enough to take care of ourselves.

That age actually comes pretty quickly. Some of us mature quickly, and some of us never mature beyond adolescent thinking. Why? There are several reasons, but unless we are mentally handicapped, none of them are anyone's fault except our own.

Million-Dollar Memo:

If confidence is the air in your tires, then excuses are the potholes that leave you with four flats—and no spare—on your journey to invention.

Avoiding the Blame Game

To be successful you must be self-reliant. Know yourself; trust yourself. It is fine to seek mentorship, advice, and even physical labor from outside sources—indeed, you'll soon have to do all three—but at the end of the day the proper care and feeding of your own success starts and stops with you.

We make excuses to make ourselves feel better, forgetting that excuses only hurt the person making them. Florence Nightingale once said, "I attribute my success to this: I never gave or took an excuse." Be like Florence Nightingale and "nurse" yourself back to a place of confidence, where excuses are not only not heard, they're unheard of.

We often feel we can get by with blaming others for all we have not become. It's our parents fault because they divorced when we were three. It's our spouse's fault because he or she doesn't support us. It's our children's fault because we have no time for ourselves. It's our neighbor's fault because he borrowed the tool you were going to use to finally start building your invention.

Well, I've got some enlightening news for you: no one cares. If your parents broke up when you were three, confront them, hash it out, and then move on. If your spouse or kids aren't giving you enough time to devote to your invention, explain its importance to your joint future and I'm sure they'll see the light! And if your neighbor borrowed your tool set, don't wait for him to return it before starting to build your dreams—walk across the street and get it back!

Say it with me: no one cares. People may sympathize with you from time to time, but trust me: no one really cares enough to disrupt their daily routine. People are not going to slow down and stop doing what they are doing so they can pick you up and carry you to the finish line.

That's why you have to rely on yourself to run the race alone. You may start in the pack and follow the herd at first, but as the race wears on people drop off, and there you are, running down the middle of the course all alone.

What will you do then, without people pacing you or handing you cups of water or urging you on? You can't quit just because your fan club takes a cat nap; you've got to run the race even when no one's screaming your name or urging you on.

In fact, much of the race will be run to the sounds of something far different from cheering. I can guarantee you that many people are going to "make fun" of you and your idea when they first hear about it. Don't let them shake your confidence; stay the course no matter how great, or how bad, people tell you you're doing.

People I considered my "friends" from work would often ask me how the project was going. It was amazing to me how, when I gave *some* of them good news, they seemed to almost cringe with disappointment—but when I responded with a recent setback, they would express glee.

I am asking you to shake off that baggage and get into the game—anyway. Remember all your excuses and walk up to the finish line—anyway. Put the blame game behind you and prepare for the journey—anyway. And once you start, make your dream happen *any way* you can.

My hope is this book will help you accomplish your dream. But remember, no matter how much help you find on these pages, your dream will never become a reality without that one important ingredient: *you.*

Million-Dollar Memo:

We make excuses to make ourselves feel better, forgetting that excuses only hurt the person making them.

Step #4

✦

Understand Patents and Prototypes

Whoever invents or discovers any new and useful process, machine, manufacture, or composition of matter, or any new and useful improvement thereof, may obtain a patent

—Section 101, United States Code, 1988

Congratulations! Since you have not stopped reading this book, you must have decided you have what it takes. That is a huge step, and I am pleased you have decided to take it! The best part is that we're just getting to the "good" part: patents and prototypes. This is where the journey starts to gain some recognizable accomplishments.

The subject of patents and prototypes can be daunting at first, but I've got a quick way for you to think of them: *paperwork* and *practice*. In the case of the ShurTrax patent, I followed a template when filing the provisional patent for myself. As for your patent, well, we'll get into that a lot heavier later on, but for now think of filing for your patent as *paperwork*; lots of paperwork.

Merriam-Webster defines a prototype as "an original model on which something is patterned." I'll flesh this description out a little further in this chapter, but for now, think of a prototype as a model you can *practice* on. For instance, my prototype for ShurTrax allowed me to test the ballast out in my very own truck. So don't be discouraged by the forms, definitions, and examples in this, our longest section so far. Inventing your dream can be as simple as the 2 P's: *paperwork* (patent) and *practice* (prototype).

Now, aren't you glad you stuck around?

Million-Dollar Memo:

The subject of patents and prototypes can be daunting at first, but I've got a quick way for you to think of them: paperwork and practice.

What is a Patent?

According to United States Patent and Trademark Office (http://www.uspto.gov/), "a patent for an invention is the grant of a property right to the inventor, issued by the United States Patent and Trademark Office. Generally, the term of a new patent is twenty years from the date on which the application for the patent was filed in the United States or, in special cases, from the date an earlier related application was filed, subject to the payment of maintenance fees. U.S. patent grants are effective only within the United States, U.S. territories, and U.S. possessions. Under certain circumstances, patent term extensions or adjustments may be available.

"The right conferred by the patent grant is, in the language of the statute and of the grant itself, 'the right to exclude others from making, using, offering for sale, or selling' the invention in the United States or 'importing' the invention into the United States. What is granted is not the right to make, use, offer for sale, sell, or import, but the right to exclude others from making, using, offering for sale, selling, or importing the invention. Once a patent is issued, the patentee must enforce the patent without aid of the USPTO.

"There are three types of patents:

1. **Utility patents** may be granted to anyone who invents or discovers any new and useful process, machine, article of manufacture, or composition of matter, or any new and useful improvement thereof;

2. **Design patents** may be granted to anyone who invents a new, original, and ornamental design for an article of manufacture; and

3. **Plant patents** may be granted to anyone who invents or discovers and asexually reproduces any distinct and new variety of plant."

Million-Dollar Memo:

"A patent for an invention is the grant of a property right to the inventor, issued by the United States Patent and Trademark Office." (http://www.uspto.gov/)

Patience, Patents, and Procedure

Before filing my own provisional patent, I read up on patents thoroughly. What is a provisional patent? According to USPTO Web site, "Since June 8, 1995, the United States Patent and Trademark Office (USPTO) has offered inventors the option of filing a provisional application for patent which was designed to provide a lower-cost first patent filing in the United States."

At first, I was just as confused as you may be right now! I needed to find out everything from "do I need one?" to "which one(s) do I need?" Fortunately, I found a company on the Internet called Jacob Enterprises Inc. that offered some literature guides. I purchased two of them, *The Inventor's Knowledge Guide* and *Provisional Patent Application Guide*, both of which I highly recommend.

From these two great resources I found out all I needed to know about which patents were needed and how to file them. They put to rest a lot of my fears, and I even discovered that I could write my idea down with pencil and paper and have a notary notarize my idea; this would give me immediate protection until I could file a provisional patent by myself and achieve "patent pending" status—for only $80.

This would last one year, which would give me enough time to decide if I wanted to spend $4,000 to have a patent attorney file a non-provisional utility patent that would last another twenty years from the filing date.

I decided to first notarize and then file for provisional patent protection. (At the end of this chapter I provide an actual template and my original provisional patent application for the reader to use when filing their own provisional patent.)

This made so much sense to me. The $80 fee (which has been increased since I filed my provisional patent) bought me one year to do patent searches (patent attorneys do this for approximately $400) to make sure I wasn't infringing on someone else and to see if the ShurTrax products were worth pursuing.

For less than $500, I was on my way!

Care to join me?

Million-Dollar Memo:

"The option of filing a provisional application for patent ... was designed to provide a lower-cost first patent filing in the United States." (http://www.uspto.gov/)

Protecting Your Idea:
Three Reasons Why It's Easier Than You Think

Patent, copyright, trademark, infringement, settlement, lawsuit—the list of inventor concerns goes on and on, but having been through the process, I can tell you this much: it's all much ado about nothing.

People sometimes mistakenly think someone is lurking around the corner, waiting to steal their ideas before they get a chance to patent them. After going through this process I can see how silly those fears are.

There are several reasons why people won't steal your idea:

1. **Cost:** The cost of pioneering a new product is higher than I ever imagined—and a huge turnoff to would-be scammers.

2. **Time:** It takes three to five years before a normal product becomes profitable. Naturally, big companies prefer to wait until a product shows high profit margins before they get interested, and they would rather pay big dollars for a proven product than develop an idea that may or may not succeed.

3. **Energy:** The same big companies' decision makers who hold the purse strings usually lack the energy or resources necessary to invest in developing a new product. In corporate America, reputations hinge on these types of decisions.

Million-Dollar Memo:

People sometimes mistakenly think someone is lurking around the corner, waiting to steal their ideas before they get a chance to patent them. After going through this process, I can see how silly those fears are.

The Prototype:
Big Models for Bigger Kids!

Once I had put my mind at ease with investing in a provisional patent, another Internet search turned up a company in Tennessee that would take my crude drawings and make a prototype ShurTrax bladder for me. They would do so using a technology called radio frequency welding.

I wanted to limit the number of sizes I would have to make to fit cars, compact trucks, and full-size trucks. To accomplish this, I would need three sizes designed to fit snugly in the beds of short-bed pickups. This would allow for fewer inventories when I got into the distribution mode.

I got back online to calculate the height of the ShurTrax. I calculated the height the product would need to be for the added weight by measuring the square inches and converting it on a table, using eight pounds per gallon (the approximate weight of water) in the equation. I determined the ShurTrax would have to hold three inches of water in height to be effective.

I then went to work in my basement, cutting and taping cardboard into configurations that I eventually placed in the back of people's trucks while running around the neighborhood making sure the full-size model would fit all full-size pickups.

When I received the prototype, I was extremely excited. Can you imagine? My idea had moved from my head, to paper, to prototype in only three months time. I immediately installed the product in my pickup. Once again, the timing was just right; there was a perfect, slick snow falling in central Ohio. I jumped in the truck and headed down the road like a kid with a new toy.

It worked like magic. No more slipping or sliding! I'm not kidding; my truck was performing unbelievably. I knew for the first time I was really onto something. I drove back home and saw my neighbor standing in his garage, so I went to work immediately on my marketing campaign.

Million-Dollar Memo:

Can you imagine? My idea had moved from my head, to paper, to prototype in only three months time.

Questions, Answers, and Feedback:
The Inventor's Battle Cry

When big companies do research on what flavors of ice cream appeal to the public, how hot to make a toasted sub, or even what to call the next big baby doll, they use something called a focus group.

Focus groups are also available to inventors, at a costly price. Focus groups bring in a sample of the population that could be affected by your product and basically do "show and tell" sessions in hopes of getting you some needed feedback. Since I didn't have the money to pay for this service, I decided once again this was something I could do on my own.

Once you get a prototype, don't only try it out for yourself, but immediately start collecting the opinions of others. Really ask—and listen—for responses both positive and negative. Don't hide your ears when people start giving you the "yeah, but ..." test; listen and fix the problem, if there is one.

Remember, it's much better to hear about, respond to, and fix the problem now—after investing a few hundred bucks and just as many hours—than later on down the road when the investment is thousands of dollars and your blood, sweat, and tears!

Fortunately, my neighbor I saw standing in his garage started gushing over the ShurTrax and said he wanted one for his truck. That was the exact response I was looking for.

Eager to keep the positive momentum rolling, I let Todd Walker, a young manufacturing engineer at work, in on what I was doing. He was more than happy to help and became very helpful to this project in several ways. This was another great lesson I can't help but share: don't just let others give advice—let them get their hands dirty. Use your resources, which don't always include money. If you have friends with particular experience that you need—such as a lawyer, handyman, marketing whiz, or mechanical engineer—approach them about helping you. Remember, as the old saying goes, "All they can say is no!"

Of course, as excited as I was, I knew that it was best to proceed with caution. I didn't want to get too far ahead of myself too fast, so I made sure to take it step-by-step, all according to plan. I can't think of better advice for you.

So before moving past this point, several questions about the product must be answered by not only the inventor, but friends and relatives as well. Be very critical of your product when doing the following exercise. Remember, the only person that will be hurt if you proceed with a bad idea is you. Some of these questions are used by potential infomercial companies as a way to see if your product will sell. (We'll talk more about infomercials later.)

Ask yourself these questions:

- Does your product solve a problem?

- Does your product have unique features and/or benefits?

- Can your product produce a profit margin of 50 percent for you and more margins for your distribution process and still have an appealing sale price to the customer?

- Can your product be retailed and distributed in a package that is not too large? (Large packages eat up shipping trailer, warehouse, and retail floor space.)

- Is your product safety-related? (Not necessary, but certainly helps—people pay for safety.)

- How big is your market potential?

Million-Dollar Memo:

Once you get a prototype, don't only try it out for yourself, but immediately start collecting the opinions of others.

Forms and Figures

Paperwork is something the would-be inventor should get used to—and quick. Ideas might be the fuel that keeps an invention chugging toward the marketplace, but paperwork—and plenty of it—lines the path to that very first sale.

On the following pages you will find several forms necessary to fill out your patent request. I have included several blank forms, and one form filled-in with my own personal information to show you how simple it is.

Again, "simple" is a relative term. I found the forms easier to fill out because I'd done so much homework. By the time you finish this book, they will look less intimidating to you as well.

Finally, please don't follow my lead just because you're reading this book; do what you need to do to make yourself feel comfortable—and market your invention your own way. But know that the more you know about the process, the more you *can* do yourself.

Million-Dollar Memo:

Ideas might be the fuel that keeps an invention chugging toward the marketplace, but paperwork—and plenty of it—lines the path to that very first sale.

In The United States Patent and Trademark Office

Inventor: _____

Residence: _____

Title: _____

Commissioner of Patents and Trademarks
Washington, D.C. 20231

Provisional Patent Application Cover Sheet

Transmitted herewith for filing is the provisional patent application of: _____

_____.

1.) Enclosed are:

[ ] _____ Page specification.

[ ] _____ Sheet(s) of drawings.

[ ] 1 page Small Entity Statement.

[ ] Other (Please Describe) _____

[ ] Postcard for acknowledgment.

2.) Fee Payment: _____.

[ ] Enclosed is a check payable to the Commissioner of Patents and Trademarks

[ ] The Commissioner is hereby authorized to charge any additional fees required or credit any overpayment to my own personal _____ credit card with numbers _____with expira-

tion date of _____and with the name of

_____.

3.) Please recognize the following citizen of the United States of America:, as the inventor in this matter and send the filing receipt and any other correspondence to him at the address given below:

_____

_____

_____

_____

4.) The subject invention was not made by an agency of the United States Government or under a contract with an agency of the United States Government.

Respectfully submitted,

_____

Place your signature here

_____

Print name and address

CERTIFICATION UNDER 37 CFR 1.10 I hereby certify that this Provisional Application and the documents referred to as enclosed therein are being deposited with the United States Postal Service on this date, _____ in an envelope as "Express Mail Post Office to Addressee" Mailing Label Number _____ addressed to the Commissioner of Patents and Trademarks, Washington, D.C.

PROVISIONAL PATENT APPLICATION

Inventor:.
Title:.

Specification

Background/Problem

_____
_____
_____

Solution

_____
_____
_____

Drawings

_____
_____
_____

Detailed Description

_____
_____
_____

Attachments:

Verified Statement (Declaration) Claiming Small Entity Status
(37 Cfr 1.9(F) And 1.27(B)-Independent Inventor

As a below named inventor, I hereby declare that I qualify as an independent inventor as defined in 37 CFR 1.9(d) for purposes of paying reduced fees under Section 41(a) and (b) of Title 35, United States Code, to the Patent and Trademark Office with regard to the invention entitled:

_____

by inventor(s): _____
described in:

[ ] the specification filed herewith
[ ] application serial no., filed
[ ] patent no., issued

I have not assigned, granted, conveyed or licensed and am under no obligation under contract or law to assign, grant conveyor license, any rights to the invention to any person who could not qualify as an independent inventor under 37 CFR 1.9(d) if that person had made the invention, or to any concern which would not qualify as a small business concern under 37 CFR 1.9(d) or a nonprofit organization under 37 CFR 1.9(e).

Each person, concern or organization to which I have assigned, granted, conveyed, or licensed or am under an obligation under contract or law to assign, grant, convey, or license any rights in the invention is listed below:

[ ] no such person, concern, or organization
[ ] persons, concerns or organizations listed below

I acknowledge the duty to file, in this application or patent, notification of any change in status resulting in loss of entitlement to small entity status prior to paying, or at the time of payment, the earliest of the issue fee or any maintenance fee due after the date on which status as a small business entity is no longer appropriate.
(37 CFR 1.28(b)).

I hereby declare that all statements made herein of my own knowledge are true and that all statements made on information and belief are believed to be true; and further that these statements were made with the knowledge that willful false statements and the like so made are punishable by fine or imprisonment, or both, under Section 1001 of Title 18 of the United States Code, and that such willful false statements may jeopardize the validity of the application, any patent issuing thereon, or any patent to which this verified statement is directed.

_____

Name of first inventor

_____

Signature of inventor

_____

Date

(Small Entity—Independent Inventor)

- Note: *The following eight pages illustrate my actual Provisional Patent Application filed for ShurTrax (with my personal information "x"ed out).*

I hope you find this a useful template if you decide to file your provisional patent for yourself.

Marty

In The United States Patent and Trademark Office

Inventor: <u>Marty J. Carty</u>
Residence: <u>xxx, Ohio xxxxx</u>
Title: <u>Water filled pickup truck bed mat</u>

Commissioner of Patents and Trademarks
Washington, D.C. 20231

Provisional Patent Application Cover Sheet

Transmitted herewith for filing is the provisional patent application of: <u>Marty J. Carty</u>

1) Enclosed are:

   (x) 4 page specification.

   (x) 2 sheets of drawings.

   (x) 1 page Small Entity Statement.

   (x) Post card for acknowledgement.

2) Fee Payment: $80.00

   (x) Enclosed is a check payable to the Commissioner of Patents and Trademarks

   (x) The Commissioner is hereby authorized to charge any additional fees required or credit any overpayment to my personal xxxx credit card with numbers xxx xxxx xxxx xxxx with expiration date of xx/xx and with the name of Marty J. Carty.

3) Please recognize the following citizen of the United States of America: Marty J. Carty, as the inventor in this matter and send the filing receipt and any other correspondence to him at the address given below:

Marty J. Carty

123 Xxxx Drive

Xxxx, Ohio xxxxx

Telephone Numbers: (Home) xxx-xxx-xxxx (Cell) xxx-xxx-xxxx (Work) xxx-xxx-xxxx

4) The subject invention was not made by an agency of the United States Government or under a contract with an agency of the United States Government.

Respectfully submitted,

Marty J. Carty

Marty J. Carty, 123 Xxxx Drive Xxxx, Ohio xxxxx

CERTIFICATION UNDER 37 CFR 1.10 I hereby certify that this Provisional Application and the documents referred to as enclosed therein are being deposited with the United States Postal Service on this date, 12/17/02 in an envelope as "Express Mail Post to Addressee" Mailing Label Number addressed to the Commissioner of Patents and Trademarks, Washington, D.C.

PROVISIONAL PATENT APPLICATION

Inventor: Marty J. Carty
Title: Water filled pickup truck bed mat

<u>Specification</u>

Background/Problem

Every winter season pickup truck owners are faced with a dilemma. What are they going to put in the bed of their trucks to add weight? Sandbags, wood chunks, concrete blocks, or snow is often used. The installations of these current solutions are not easy. These current solutions also roll around and/or prevent the owner from hauling other objects in their truck during the winter months. The sandbags, wood chunks, and concrete blocks also have huge safety concerns. These types of objects could become potentially harmful projectiles in the case of an accident.

Solution

Pickup truck owners would appreciate the easy installation of the water filled pickup truck bed mat. In the autumn the owner would place the mat into his or her truck and fill with water. In the spring the mat could be easily drained, rolled up, and put away in storage until the next autumn. The water mat would be no more than 3" high and lay flat in the truck bed. The construction of the mat would also allow the owner to haul other objects in the truck during the winter without having the current weight methods in their way. The mat would consist of a rubber bladder and a vinyl protective covering. If the water were to freeze, the rubber mat would expand without busting. A winterizing liquid may be added to prevent freezing.

Drawings

One exemplary embodiment of the subject invention disclosed in this specification is shown in the attached drawings, wherein:

Fig. 1 is a top view of the water mat. This view illustrates the mat lying in a full-size truck bed. The listed size is 4' × 8'. This view shows the mat being rectangle in dimension. The final shape and size of the water mat is yet to be determined. The fill plug and drain plugs are both pictured in the right rear corner next to tailgate. The fill plug will be on the topside of mat and the drain plug on the bottom or under side of the mat.

Fig. 2 is a side view of the water mat. This shows the mat as being 2" in height. The actual height may be from 2" to 4". The interior of the mat may require rubber baffles. The fill plug is pictured on the top and the drain plug on the bottom or underside of the mat. The liquid being pictured inside the mat is water.

Detailed Description

In the following description, like reference characters designate like or corresponding parts throughout the several views. Also, in the following description, it is understood that terms such as "forward", "rearward", "left", "right", "upwardly", "downwardly", and the like, are words of convenience and are not construed to be limiting terms.

Now referring to the drawings of figs. 1 and 2, there is shown a water filled mat generally designated by the numeral 10, being constructed in accordance with the principles of the present invention. The water mat 10, basically comprises an outer sheath 12, an inner sheath 14, and a liquid filler material 16 disposed within the inner sheath 14, and in the embodiment shown, the water mat 10 takes on the characteristic shape of a flat rectangular mat, however, other similar shapes are envisioned. The outside sheath 12 of the water mat 10 is composed of a rugged fabric material, such as vinyl or canvas material, which doesn't tear easily when cargo is loaded on top of it. The inner sheath 14 of the water mat 10 is composed of a rubber material, which is thick enough not to allow water to freeze and bust it. The inner filler material 16 of the water mat 10 is composed of a flexible sponge-like material to serve as a water baffle, however a similar mat without the inner filler 16 is envisioned.

The inventor has discovered that a rubber mat with a vinyl protective coating would allow the owners of pickup trucks to haul cargo with the water mat installed. The water mat is to be placed in the bed of pickup trucks for adding weight in winter driving conditions. An 8' x 4' x 2" mat consists of 9216 cubic inches. This would allow the rubber mat to hold 39.89 gallons of water. Water weighs 8 lbs per gallon for a total liquid weight of approximately 320 lbs. The weight of the water mat material could push the total weight to over 350 lbs when mat is full of water. The rubber inner bladder must be thick enough that water when frozen would not bust the material. A winterizing liquid being added is envisioned.

Attachments:

2 sheet drawings with 2 figures.

Small Entity Status Form

Verified Statement (Declaration) Claiming Small Entity Status (37 Cfr 1.9(F) And 1.27 (B)—Independent Inventor

As a below named inventor, I hereby declare that I qualify as an independent inventor as Defined in 37 CFR 1.9(d) for purposes of paying reduced fees under Section 41(a) and (b) of Title 35, United States Code, to the Patent and Trademark Office with regard to the invention Entitled: Water filled pickup truck bed mat

By inventor: Marty J. Carty
Described in:

(x) the specification filed herewith
( ) application serial no., filed
( ) patent no., issued

I have not assigned, granted, conveyed or licensed and am under no obligation under contract or law to assign, grant conveyor license, any rights to the invention to any person who could not qualify as an independent inventor under 37 CFR 1.9(d) if that person had mad the invention, or to any concern which would not qualify as a small business concern under 37 CFR 1.9(d) or a nonprofit organization under 37 CFR 1.9(e).

Each person, concern or organization to which I have assigned, granted, conveyed, or licensed or am under an obligation under contract or law to assign, grant, convey, or license any rights in the invention is listed below:

(x) no such person, concern, or organization
( ) persons, concerns or organizations listed below

I acknowledge the duty to file, in this application or patent, notification of any change in status resulting in loss of entitlement to small entity status prior to paying, or at the time of payment, the earliest of the issue fee or any maintenance fee due after the date on which status as a small business entity is no longer appropriate. (37 CFR 1.28(b)).

I hereby declare that all statements made herein of my own knowledge are true and that all statements made on information and belief are believed to be true; and further that these statements were mad with the knowledge that willful false statements and the like so made are punishable by fine or imprisonment, or both, under Section 1001 of Title 18 of the United States Code, and that such willful false statements may jeopardize the validity of the application, any patent issuing thereon, or any patent to which this verified statement is directed.

Name of first inventor: Marty J. Carty

Signature of inventor:

Date: 12/17/02

(Small Entity—Independent Inventor)

Is There Ever a Perfect Time to Follow a Dream?

As you can see by these forms and the actual provisional patent application I filed, this is another piece of the process that can easily be completed by the inventor. I hope you find it helpful if you decide to file for your provisional patent yourself.

Once your provisional patent is filed, you will need to contact a patent attorney to begin the process of conducting a patent search. The results of the search will give your patent attorney the information he or she needs when filing your non-provisional patent a year from now.

I realize that this process can be pretty daunting. I encourage you to keep going. The steps of the process are very clear and I'm going to continue leading you through them, step-by-step. Don't stop now!

It can be easy to get discouraged and think that the time isn't right; that this is too challenging or complicated or expensive or futile. It is and it isn't; it's all of those things, but all of those things are definitely worth it! This may not be the perfect time for you to create your invention, but was last month? Last week? Last year? When *is* the perfect time to follow your dream?

I say there is no perfect time, so you might as well start now!

Million-Dollar Memo:

The results of the patent search will give your patent attorney the information he or she needs when filing your non-provisional patent a year from now.

Step #5

✦

Raise Capital

Lack of money is no obstacle. Lack of an idea is an obstacle.

—Ken Hakuta

Inventors face many challenges on the road to market: frustration, self-doubt, naysayers, failing the "yeah, but ..." test, insecurity, and dozens of other obstacles. Few of these obstacles are as big as the constant and never-ending quest to *raise capital.*

Money: it drives both the inventor and the consumer. Inventors want to make money; consumers want to save money. How do you do one and still accomplish the other? Even if money isn't your main priority for bringing your idea to market, you're still going to need plenty of it to bring the idea to market in the first place.

Another challenge is that idea people are rarely money people. Few of us went to Harvard Business School or even took anything as basic as Negotiating 101, so it's hard enough for us to ask for money, let alone manage it.

Remember what I said earlier in this book about making excuses? Now is not the time to let bad money management or a lack of crack negotiating skills sink your great invention. Don't complain or give up because you're "no good with money." Instead, *get* good with money—and make that dream happen!

Modern inventors must be both idea people *and* business people. Raising capital isn't a bonus step or "extra" added benefit; it is one of the seven steps of the invention process. To skip one of these steps is to make the others harder to achieve—and to skip this step in particular is to make your dream *impossible* to achieve.

I don't know about you, but I didn't go to school to get an economics degree, and once I developed the ShurTrax prototype there was no extra time to go back to school and take classes in Raising Capital 101. All I know is what I learned along my own incredible journey to invention—and that is what I share with you now.

Million-Dollar Memo:

Inventors want to make money; consumers want to save money. How do you do one and still do the other?

Gut-Check Time

If you're like most people on this planet, you are really only dealing with two loans at any one time: your mortgage payment (loan #1) and your car payment (loan #2). Other loans that the average citizen comes across in a lifetime are student loans, a luxury loan like paying for a boat, Jet Ski, snowmobile, or other "luxury," or even putting something on layaway.

Either way, most of us are inexperienced when it comes to loans. And, the bigger the loan, the more that inexperience shows. Up until this point in my own invention process, the above types of loans were the bulk of my financial experience.

So far I'd managed to do it all myself. From researching on the Internet to paying for my own provisional patent filing to funding the prototype, I'd reached out to friends, the library, and into my own pocket to make this dream a reality.

But at some point, inspiration, perspiration, handy friends, helpful neighbors, and even elbow grease isn't enough—you are going to need to raise some extra capital. Once the patent and prototype step had been mastered, I found myself at a crossroads: my money (borrowed and savings) was beginning to run out. I needed to put together a business plan to see if I could raise some needed capital. One of the simplest, but far from minor, decisions was to turn to the bank.

I eventually took out two loans, in the amount of $12,500, from the local Citi-Financial at 20 percent interest. These were not business loans; they were personal—and they felt personal. Up until now, the idea kind of took care of itself. It required time, energy, and effort, but nothing I couldn't lose—until I took out this money.

It may not sound like a lot in the grand scheme of things, but these loans were the first risk (of many) I took. Looking back, I can't believe I did it, but without doing it I would not have progressed. I did not have the money to continue to fund this out of my pocket, but if I stopped then, I may never have restarted. It was gut-check time, and I took the plunge....

Million-Dollar Memo:

At some point, inspiration, perspiration, handy friends, helpful neighbors, and even elbow grease isn't enough—you are going to need to raise some extra capital.

Investors May Be Closer Than You Think:
Five Tips for Finding Funds

Borrowing from the bank made sense for me at the time, but it was just one of several strategies I would eventually use to fund the invention, creation, and marketing of the ShurTrax System. Here are my top five options for funding your own inventing process:

1. **Your rainy day is here:** I always suggest starting from where you are. In this case, look to your own savings, investments, and even home equity before you seek outside funding. This may not be enough to last the full course of the invention process, but it's a great place to start. What can you do, personally, to fund your invention? It may be piecemeal, a few hundred dollars at a time. It may require larger draws on your savings and investments as time goes on. By no means do I suggest wiping your savings out entirely to get started, but I do recommend sitting down and crunching the numbers to see how much you can comfortably afford to contribute yourself.

2. **Banks and financial institutions:** Banks are great, but don't trust them blindly or get bullied into borrowing x dollars when you only need y dollars. Just like you research patents, procedures, and prototypes, make sure that you study options at a variety of banks for a variety of figures; then make the choice that is best for *you*.

3. **Friends and family:** Another great place to start is by talking to family and friends. Perhaps your parents or siblings have expressed interest in "helping you out." Don't be shy,

or even proud; let them help you! If they haven't offered, ask them anyway. Don't be disappointed if and when they say no. Be patient, but be persistent; many will invest once you get a little farther down the road. My parents and one brother eventually became investors in ShurTrax.

4. **Private investors:** Investors can get tricky, even when they're in your own family, or from just up the street. Start local before branching out. Who do you know, locally, who might want to invest in your product? What can they offer you? What can you offer them? Talk to people—nothing's official until it's in a contract and both parties have signed. Test the waters and let people know you're looking for investors. Be very careful here, but don't rule out the possibility that someone, or several someones, might want to contribute to the cause.

5. **Partners:** If all of your resources have been exhausted and you still need more money to cross the finish line, consider the admittedly major decision of finding a partner to purchase a portion of your company. It may not be the ideal situation, but if it means the difference between giving up on your project for lack of funds and crossing the finish line with a business partner, which choice do you think makes the most sense? (See next section.)

Million-Dollar Memo:

By no means do I suggest wiping your savings out entirely to get started, but I do recommend sitting down and crunching the numbers to see how much you can comfortably afford to contribute yourself.

Two Checkbooks Are Better Than One

Sometimes life works in mysterious ways. Even with my own savings, contributing every extra penny, taking out two loans, and budgeting down to the nickel, I came to yet another cross-roads on my journey.

I was now completely out of money, inventory, and time. The year was quickly passing and I needed $4,000 to pay my patent attorney to file the non-provisional patent for me by the end of December 2003.

Where would I turn?

What would I do?

The Marines have a saying; I suppose it's more like a slogan: "Improvise, Adapt, and Overcome." Who better to listen to than the Marines when you're trying to best an insurmountable challenge, right?

Coincidentally, my older brother Dan had a position with a company in Tennessee called Murray Inc. that made outdoor power equipment. When I discussed some of the challenges I was having securing funding for the next leg of my journey, Dan was kind enough to have his consultant, Jim Brooks, look at ShurTrax and let him know I may be looking for a business partner.

Then fortune smiled on me again. Jim Brooks not only liked the ShurTrax concept, but it just so happened he lived only nine miles from me! Sometimes the planets just need to align for you. This was certainly one of those times.

I decided it was time to pick up the phone and call Jim Brooks to see if he had any interest in buying into the company. I thought it would be a great fit, since I knew manufacturing and he knew sales and marketing. I didn't realize at the time how crucial it was to land a guy like Jim.

I went to Jim's office and he was genuinely interested in diving in. Jim was in his mid-fifties and tired of working for others. He wanted to spend his last years before retirement devoting energy into his own product. We agreed that I would sell 49 percent of my company to Jim, and as we raised future capital we would sell shares equally and put the money back into the business.

Looking back, I can see how fortunate I was to run across Jim. In your own search for a partner, remember that it must be a good fit; Jim has ended up being the perfect fit. I have had several things go wrong in this process, but the rightness of this move more than makes up for all those wrong turns along the way.

Million-Dollar Memo:

Sometimes the planets just need to align for you. This was certainly one of those times.

It's Your *First* Company—Not Your *Only*

Thomas Edison held a world record of 1,093 patents for inventions such as the phonograph, light bulb, and motion pictures. Benjamin Franklin's experiments with a kite in a thunderstorm led to the development of the lightning rod. He also invented bifocal glasses and the Franklin stove.

As idea people, we too must be passionate, prolific, and proactive; we can't be shortsighted. Don't think of this as your only idea, but one of many. Don't think of this as your only company, but your first.

My rule of thumb for someone starting their own company with little money is to be prepared to sell off a majority of your first company to experience the payday we're all after. Absolutes are rare in the idea process; they're even rarer in the funding process. Don't think of 100 percent as success—think of success as success! When the day comes that your product is on the market, being used by American consumers and actually turning a profit, you will have done well if you still own 20 percent of the company.

Anything more than that is exceptional!

You might think that partnering up with Jim Brooks was a great payday for me, and it was, but I did not get to keep any of the proceeds from selling 49 percent of the company. However, it did allow me to pay off my previous loans and file my patent on time. The rest of the money went into the company for our daily cash needs.

But in the final analysis, this *was* a huge payday for me. I knew profit was a long way off; my success came in stages. Simply getting the idea off the ground was a success; filing the provisional patent and getting a prototype made was another.

Finding Jim was yet one more in a long line of successes—one that no bank or lending institution could put a price tag on.

A high school friend of mine was an attorney, so I called on him to take my business plan and create a company for me to operate under. I chose the name SealPak Innovations LTD. The LTD stands for limited partnership. I chose this name, because I looked at ShurTrax as the lead product only. I envisioned SealPak Innovations as being a company that brought forth many new innovative products and packaging services.

Although our Series A Investors later asked us to convert the LTD to SealPak Innovations Inc., I still recommend starting a company as a limited partnership. There are some tax advantages and fewer liabilities for beginning a company this way.

LTD companies offer units instead of stock when you begin to sell percentages of the company to raise working capital. Jim and I realized we needed to begin selling units (each unit equals one percent of the company). Now we needed to determine what a unit was worth.

Ray Hamilton is a lifelong friend of my parents. He is a semi-retired accountant in Michigan, and he heard about what I was doing. He called me and wanted to help. I told Ray we needed to raise capital, but wasn't sure how to set the price per unit. I then offered him a price per unit and he wisely said, "That is not enough, but I will give you five times that amount per unit." Talk about a dear friend of the family.

Without Ray helping establish a fair price per unit, we would have given away too much of the company too soon.

Million-Dollar Memo:

As idea people, we too must be passionate, prolific, and proactive; we can't be shortsighted. Don't think of this as your only idea, but one of many. Don't think of this as your only company, but your first.

Beware the Venture Capitalists

You'll recall that earlier in this chapter I mentioned five great ways to find funding for your project. Notice I didn't include "venture capital" on that list! What is venture capital? According to www.wikipedia.org, "Venture capital is a type of private equity capital typically provided by outside investors for financing new, growing, or struggling businesses. Venture capital investments are generally high-risk investments but offer the potential for above-average returns and/or a percentage of ownership of the company."

If only I'd followed my own advice. My own mingling with venture capital soon became one of the largest mistakes we made as a company. But hindsight is twenty-twenty, and when capital is short, and needs are many, sometimes even the longest shots start to seem more and more reasonable.

Case in point: one day I received a call from a guy—we'll call him "Chad"—who had "heard about ShurTrax" and wanted to meet me "immediately." He said he could introduce me to venture capitalists who could inject all the money we needed into the company within two weeks.

Six months later, I turned down the only "offer" Chad ever brought to us. It's in quotation marks because I don't know if you can even call it an offer. The venture capitalists were asking to take over our company and give us no money. In return, they would fund future needs "as they saw fit." As for running the company, "Chad" and the venture group would take majority ownership from Jim and me—*and* take control of the company.

I realize now the plan was to starve Jim and I to the point where we would fall for this—or risk losing the company for lack of cash. If anyone ever approaches you with a phone cord in each ear, slick talking, and full of promises, turn and run away immediately!

Chad ended up taking us to arbitration after we did receive money from other groups. They said our contract stated we owed them $25,000 for their past efforts. Even though they totally abandoned us after that offer, the arbitrator ruled they were allowed to do that and we lost the case.

Like I said, *run*!

Million-Dollar Memo:

If anyone ever approaches you with a phone cord in each ear, slick talking, and full of promises, turn and run away immediately!

From Devils to Angels—A Payoff with Wings!

Life is a series of extremes. From cold to hot, from hard to soft, from blue skies to gray, it's hard to appreciate one extreme without the other. Raising capital is no different; Jim and I soon went from one extreme to the other!

Dabbling with venture capital ended up costing us money in the long run, so my business partner and I decided we needed a new strategy. Little did we know it involved wings! On a tip, I discovered the e-mail address of a guy I'll call Justin, the president of the Ohio TechAngel Fund LLC in Columbus, Ohio. I e-mailed him a business plan and PowerPoint presentation.

Justin immediately wrote me back with some pointers on things they were looking for. I made the changes and resent the files to him. He advised me to get in touch with a guy I'll call Bart. In another twist of fate, Jim and I had met Bart previously. (Jim's wife, Linda, knew Bart.)

So, we called Bart and he liked what we had to say. Eventually, we hired him to represent us with three Ohio Angel Funds. Bart knew the key players and had chaired a state committee that offered a 25 percent state tech tax credit to any approved Ohio resident who invested in an approved Ohio company. We submitted an application and were approved as a tech investment since we had a patent-pending product.

Angel funds are called "angels" because they do not look to take over the operations of your company, unlike many venture capitalists. Angels are looking for investments where the owners are willing to build the risky business for three to five years and *then* sell the profitable company for a nice payday.

After careful consideration, that plan worked for Jim and me. Bart did an outstanding job of not only getting us funding, but doing it in record time. Thanks to his help, and several revisions of our business plan, we received $640,000 from angel funding and a $600,000 bank line! Needless to say, this eased our money woes considerably.

On a side note, I don't want the reader to think getting angel funding is easy. We were certainly in the right place at the right time, and having Bart represent us was crucial. Consider this: the Ohio TechAngel Fund (OTAF) prescreened five hundred and fifty applicants, out of which approximately fifty were allowed to present. Out of those, five received funding—and we were the only company approved that had a retail product. So the odds are stacked against you, but just as with everything else in life, the harder you work, the better your chances become.

Along with the OTAF we also received money from two other Ohio-based angel funds: QCA, or Queen City Angels, from Cincinnati, and Core Network from Toledo both piggy-backed onto the deal.

In this case, the more the merrier!

Now you may think our money problems were over. Think again! I later found out that angel-funded businesses never meet their initial sales projections—and we were no exception. After we had spent the money on inventory and advertising, we found ourselves short on cash when we failed to meet our sales quota. Thus, we had to return to the investors and ask for more money.

Advertising is a necessary evil. As you will see later in Step #6, retail stores do not sell anything. Their function is to supply to their customers what they are asking for. Your job is to create the demand through advertising.

The investors did ante up with more funding, but they took some serious hide off of Jim and me this time around. The second round of funding was based on us returning those funds to them in one year with interest. We also had to issue them warrants for additional stock. In essence they were getting their cake and eating it too. However, they would argue they were taking a bigger risk this time around and that merited this payback. Make sure that when figuring how much money you may need, you exaggerate it considerably so this does not happen to you. Obviously, you will have to justify the needed funds, but there should be a "safety net" established in the event you miss the first year's sales numbers.

Million-Dollar Memo:

Life is a series of extremes. From cold to hot, from hard to soft, from blue skies to gray, it's hard to appreciate one extreme without the other.

Step #6

✦

Establish a Pipeline

Patience, persistence, and perspiration make an unbeatable combination for success.

—Napoleon Hill

A product is nothing if there's not a pipeline to keep it flowing. It's the age-old law of supply and demand: you can't keep up with demand if you have no supply. But establishing a pipeline is more than just having product on hand; it's forming relationships with people who can help sell your product. This includes manufacturers, sales representatives, and advertisers, and everyone down to the clerks who stock the shelves and the cashiers who ring up the sales.

It amazed me how much I had to learn even *after* all I'd learned up to this point. It seemed the journey was never ending, and I'm sure it must feel the same to you right about now. But rest assured, with information like the materials found in this book and the other resources I've recommended throughout, the journey does have seven recognizable steps—and we're almost there! So if you can just stay with me a little longer, I think you'll finally see the light at the end of the tunnel.

Remember, getting the product is half the battle, so we're going to be learning about the people who can place the product as well. They are all part of the pipeline.

But the best part is, so are you!

Million-Dollar Memo:

It's the age-old law of supply and demand: you can't keep up with demand if you have no supply.

Manufacturer Migraine

Words tend to intimidate us, but to keep from getting overwhelmed it's really important not to panic when you see words like prototype, pipeline, or, as we're about to hear in this section, manufacturer.

Let the words sit and marinate for awhile, and find something comforting and a little easier to compare them to. For instance, earlier we likened the prototype to practice. For this section, let's talk about manufacturers, but refer to them in a way we can better understand. How about widget-makers?

There; that's not so bad, right? Because no matter what you're creating—be it software, hardware, a new golf club, or a color of socks, or even the ShurTrax system—you're going to have to meet some widget-makers (that is, manufacturers) along the way. Now is as good a time as any, right?

Today, creators have two main choices when it comes to getting their widgets made: domestic or international. You will probably be surprised to learn that the hardware store down the street can *not* make your invention out of scratch, no matter how long you've been friends with them or how good the boiled peanuts they make themselves in the back—and sell out front—taste.

You might have to get your widgets made as far away as three states or the opposite coast. Then again, you might find a foreign manufacturer—in this case, probably in China—to provide these widgets for you.

Which one will you choose? The choice is a personal one, but can also make or break your pipeline. Paying too much to a domestic manufacturer because you think working through China will be too complicated might eat into your bottom line longer, and harder, than you expect. Then again, simply assuming that China is the cheapest may not be correct in your instance.

Once again, do your homework. Look into options, send out feelers, ask for quotes, request samples of quality workmanship, and take this step very seriously. At this point, I was not interested in sending the manufacturing to China until I knew more about the process, evolution, and quality of the product.

Then again, I had very specific requirements of any manufacturer who would be working for me—be it foreign or domestic. For instance, there are only a handful of manufacturers in the United States with a machine platen large enough to radio frequency (RF) seal vinyl with the dimensions that ShurTrax requires. RF sealing is a process superior to "old-fashioned" heating when marrying vinyl materials together. Think of RF sealing as microwave technology. Using RF, vinyl is heated and cooled while the pressure from the press die is applied. This process only takes a matter of seconds versus minutes with heat sealing.

I also did not want to use several bar sealers and create crossing seams. I wanted the outer seal hit as one large continuous loop. To do this, a machine with a large platen was needed.

The company in Tennessee that made my prototype gave me a lead on a company in South Carolina that might be interested in making ShurTrax products. I called them and sent them the prototype. The South Carolina manufacturer said they would gladly make them. I decided I would give them a try on a few small orders, watching the quality very closely until I was satisfied. It was official; I finally had some widget makers to help me establish a pipeline.

Million-Dollar Memo:

Words tend to intimidate us, but to keep from getting over-whelmed it's really important not to panic when you see words like prototype, manufacturer, or pipeline.

Consider Cost and Retail Price

Making is a long way from selling, which is why a pipeline exists in the first place. The pipeline can be physical, as in lining up sales reps and manufacturers, but also temporal. It takes time to put all the steps into place. Just like there are seven steps to our process, as you have seen, each step of the process has its own steps within the process. So before you begin trying to sell your product, make sure you properly understand the cost structures and steps involved in getting it to market.

There are several types of distribution channels, including direct to consumer via the Internet. However, you need to price your product at a cost where you make a decent margin even if you must utilize a two- or three-step distribution process; one in which each step looks to make their expected percentage. Plus, you must save room for the final step, the retailer, to make a profit.

I mention pricing only in passing, because not only is it personal but it can be very, very perplexing. I recommend doing research on your own, both for general pricing terms and with your own potential distributors, to achieve the best plan for you and your idea or product. Every market has its own unique distribution terms and processes. Make sure you become acquainted with yours before establishing your price points.

Million-Dollar Memo:

Just like there are seven steps to our process, each step of the process has its own steps within the process.

What's in a Name?

On its way to becoming ShurTrax, my little-product-that-could had a slight identity crisis. The initial name for my product was Liqui-wate. It made sense to me, because it was liquid that filled the stabilizer, and weight—or in this case "wate"—that stabilized the truck.

Tom Erickson was the first sales rep I got to know in the pickup truck accessory market. Tom thought Liqui-wate told what the product *was*, but he reasoned that we would have more success selling it if the name told consumers what the product *does*. He suggested ShurTrax, and I quickly made the change.

Don't get hung up on sticking with your product's original name. Let your sales and marketing friends make suggestions about your product name and change your product name if they feel it will help it sell.

I did, and, looking back, I realize that ShurTrax is a lot more user-friendly than Liqui-wate might have been. But if I'd been stubborn and refused to listen to Tom, I never would have known it.

Million-Dollar Memo:

Don't get hung up on sticking with your product's original name.

When Opportunity Knocks—Be Ready!

Sometimes you have to go knocking on doors to find opportunity—and sometimes opportunity knocks on your door. When it does, be ready! Coincidentally, you may remember my brother (Dan—the brother previously mentioned) had a position with a company in Tennessee that made outdoor power equipment named Murray Inc.

Dan's job was to establish a new product line of replacement lawn mower parts. He called the new product line "Unifit," and he thought ShurTrax might fit under that umbrella since most of his customers were lawn and garden stores that sold sandbags to pickup truck owners for adding weight.

I sent him a sample and his staff thought it was worth pursuing. They asked for fifty samples of each size to test and show to their customers. Wow! I had my first customer and I needed to get some units made ASAP.

As I later discovered, tests are just that—tests. Even though I was justifiably excited about this new opportunity, I did not realize how far I had yet to go to make a test case an actual sale.

By this time I had outsourced the job of creating one hundred and eighty-six ShurTrax to be made at the company in South Carolina.

I purchased all of the necessary raw components and shipped them to South Carolina to have them sealed, packaged, and returned. Now I was finding that getting the products made and shipped to me was going to be a huge challenge! Getting the South Carolina manufacturer to deliver my products to my garage so I could ship to Murray (my brother's company) was excruciating.

Empty promises caused me to take vacation from work and head to South Carolina personally to get the units made. It worked! While personally overseeing the startup of their production, one hundred and fifty units eventually got shipped to Murray and I actually made my shipping deadline!

But now what? Now I needed to sell more; the adrenaline was really pumping! What next? It's very important during this step to not only pace yourself, but plan for yourself as well. You have to keep that pipeline flowing; that's why it's called a pipeline and not a dam! I knew the units I'd shipped to Murray were just the beginning, so I had to keep moving forward; had to keep that pipeline flowing.

So, I Googled companies that made truck accessories and started submitting product samples to them in hopes of landing a licensing agreement. A licensing agreement is what the invention companies try to accomplish for you and, basically, it is where a company does all the work and you get a royalty check for each unit sold.

I had previously decided I would start my own company and try to do the work myself to get the product to retail. If a nice licensing agreement came along, then maybe I would switch gears and turn it over to that company. The point is that I was trying all avenues. The only thing unacceptable to me was sitting and waiting for someone else to do this for me.

I soon found out that without having my product in a professional-looking package, I was wasting my time. Murray didn't mind because they had a consultant hired to design packaging for the entire Unifit line. (This consultant was Jim Brooks—remember him? He soon became my business partner in ShurTrax).

But what about the rest of the companies I'd been calling? Surely they'd want some quality packaging to help push the product, right? Well, wanting a better package and designing one are two very different things.

As you will soon read, Jim eventually was able to roll out not only attractive looking individual packaging, but floor displays for retail stores as well.

Million-Dollar Memo:

Sometimes you have to go knocking on doors to find opportunity—and sometimes opportunity knocks on your door. When it does, be ready!

If You're Not on the Web, Where Are You?
Your Very Own Storefront is a Few Clicks Away!

One of the nicer advantages of the recent communications revolution is the easy access to people through the Internet, cell phones, e-mail, and so on. These technological advances make information accessible and immediate.

Without these tools, the process of learning how and what to do would slow to a crawl. With these tools, the information is always available and just a few mouse clicks away.

Another advantage of living in this modern age is the fact you can immediately open your own store online. I opened mine by going through an Internet company called Network Solutions.

Following their step-by-step instructions, I was able to get a five-page Web site up and running for a couple hundred bucks. We later totally revamped the Web site through a professional firm, but until we had the funds, the Web site I used was very adequate.

So is time an issue for you? Have you been waiting for the right time—and the right price—to build your own Web site and start up your very own "cyber" store? With just a little research and simple instructions, you can be up and running before you can say, "Why didn't I do this sooner?"

Million-Dollar Memo:

Without these tools, the process of learning who, how, and what to do would slow to a crawl. With these tools, the information is always available and just a few mouse clicks away.

Advertising is Expensive—But It Works!
(Except When It Doesn't!)

By now the pipeline was really starting to flow. I had manufacturing and distribution in place—two big-time biggies—and was starting to see how the sales process really worked. But, still, the product was far from flying off the shelves. What now? Advertising!

Customer demand is created through advertising. When a consumer knows your product, they are more likely to buy it. Think of how you buy products, services, and ideas. The more you hear about something, the more you trust it. It's human nature.

So I started looking for ways to get some free press about my product by sending out a press release and e-mailing newspapers. My hometown paper ran a story on ShurTrax immediately, as did some national ads that ran in major newspapers. I even began to sell a few units off my Web site with this free advertising.

But you get what you pay for, and I knew I was going to have to spend some money on advertising eventually. Jim led the charge in starting to find the biggest bang for our bucks by signing a contract to advertise on the Spike TV show called *Trucks!*

While we waited for the *Trucks!* commercial to air, I decided not to let any moss grown under my feet! So I contacted the NBC news affiliate in Columbus, Ohio. Mike Jackson was a reporter that ran a weekly segment called Target 4. Mike would discuss products or other issues on this weekly installment. I e-mailed Mike and told him my story. As a result, he came over with a camera crew and interviewed me for the show.

With some newspaper stories appearing locally and nationally, now a TV news story and the Trucks! commercial under my belt, I was really starting to get the hang of this advertising strategy, right?

Wrong.

Around this time an infomercial-type company called me and asked if we would let them run our product on TV. Sounds good, right? Well, they bought our entire inventory (approximately $15,000) and promised to air the commercial one thousand times on national cable TV. All we needed to do was pay them an additional $20,000 for the filming of the sixty-second commercial and air time.

When you have little advertising money, you'll make mistakes if you try to hit a home run "on the cheap." Even though I would not say this was a total loss (we did get a DVD with a well-done commercial for that price) it certainly did not turn out the way we expected.

Listening to the infomercial sales reps, we expected them to be reordering inventory throughout the winter as they repeatedly ran the national spots. The fact is the one thousand spots they were referring to were Designated Market Areas or DMA spots. There are approximately 270 DMA spots used when 1 commercial runs nationwide. Yes, they deceived us, became almost impossible to reach, and finally provided a paper saying they aired the commercial about forty times—and most of that was in a small region of New York State. They would provide us with a monthly report showing the inventory slowly going away. We found out later they were selling our inventory on eBay. I doubt they ever sold what they were reporting back to us. Needless to say this was a huge lesson learned!

After the infomercial debacle, I immediately went back to South Carolina to get more inventory produced. On my way back, Jim called to let me know our first commercial would be airing on *Trucks!* that weekend. The results from the first airing got the phone ringing even more. It was starting to feel like a cause and effect relationship: the more we advertised, the more people knew us. The more people knew us, the more they ordered our product.

To keep the *Trucks!* theme going, we started running full-page ads in truck magazines. The little bit of TV we did worked and now we had enough funding to place full-page color ads in some of the best pickup truck enthusiast magazines. At the end of the day, we had learned a valuable lesson in keeping the pipeline full: Advertising is expensive, but necessary!

Million-Dollar Memo:

When you have little advertising money, you'll make mistakes if you try to hit a home run "on the cheap."

Let the Sales Calls Begin!

Selling is a credibility issue. The more names you can drop—this newspaper, that TV show, this radio program, that truck magazine—the easier it gets to wedge your foot in the door and actually talk to someone at some company who can buy your product! I was getting more and more excited with the free press we were still getting and decided to use these well-written, professional-looking articles to start calling on potential retail customers for the upcoming fall season.

There are several types of customers to call on. By grabbing a pickup truck accessory magazine and leafing through it, you can find several companies that sell products over the Internet and/ or Catalogs. They are all potential customers. Until you get funding and start doing some major advertising, you can forget about getting into the big box retailers. But don't be discouraged; like everything else, selling is a process. It grows slowly, but it grows. Today ShurTrax products are sold in stores throughout the United States and Canada—big stores you know and shop at—but it took time.

But even with targeting our retailer lists carefully, we once again started to hit the same obstacles with the retail people as I had with the manufacturers: our lackluster, rushed packaging didn't present the same impact as those great newspaper articles and magazine ads did.

As a result, our credibility—and potential sales—suffered. Clearly we needed to get a professional package put together. While we worked out the packaging issues, we also realized we needed to create demand. Although retailers love new products, they are not into selling—rather, they are into fulfilling their customers' demands. Once people start asking for your product, retailers will want to carry it.

So how do you create demand?

We began to do some rigorous testing on the ShurTrax units so we could answer the consumer questions that began to mount from prospective retailers. I then put together a Frequently Asked Questions, or FAQ, document and put it on our Web site. The tests included freezing and thawing, loading cargo on top of the device, and several others that we knew potential customers would be interested in.

Momentum was building, but we left no stone unturned. We did big things, like appear on TV commercials, and we did small things, like reaching out to those we could see and hear. For instance, I sold a couple units to co-workers, and they liked the product.

I then decided to cold-call a local truck accessory store called Pickups Plus. I called Larry, the owner, and asked him if I could stop by and show him this "amazing new product" and he agreed. I quickly folded, wrapped, and placed a PowerPoint insert inside a ShurTrax package and headed to the store. I even took my truck so he could see one installed. Larry came out with his son, Kyle (the store manager), and they looked it over and said they could sell these and placed an order for twelve units.

I could have skipped all the way home!

With sales growing steadily, and interest maturing right alongside our sales momentum, Jim and I realized we could no longer put off designing a better ShurTrax logo. So Jim immediately dug in on developing a professional ShurTrax logo.

We wanted something bright, colorful, memorable, and, above all, recognizable as our own. We wanted to represent

ShurTrax so that it stood out, but more than that, we wanted people to remember it. It just so happened Jim knew a freelancer that developed several ideas for the ShurTrax logo. I then called my patent attorney and had the logo registered along with the patent. It was official: not only did ShurTrax finally have professional packaging, but we also had a logo.

I like to think we picked the best one.

What do you think?

Million-Dollar Memo:

Selling is a credibility issue.

Step #7

✦

Enjoy the Pull-Through

We will always tend to fulfill our own expectation of ourselves.

—Brian Tracy

What, exactly, is pull-through? You often hear that someone "pulls through" a difficult time or sickness, but we're talking about something completely different here. When I speak of pull-through, I'm talking about sheer momentum. Pull-through is what happens when you have the complete supply chain functioning from manufacturer to end user and you're letting your customers purchases determine when and how much inventory to order.

Like generating a pipeline, pull-through is important because it is not only part of the overall invention process but also a process unto itself. You can't just ride the pull-through wave; you've got to plan, focus, and master the wave.

You may not believe this, but selling a product in and of itself will *not* make you successful. You have to know how to keep your costs low by maintaining the proper levels of inventory. After spending countless hours gaining retail space the last things you want to do is either run your retail channels out of inventory or produce too much.

Another tool in the "lean" toolbox is called Kanban. I will not go into detail about Kanban in this book; however it is a practice of letting the downstream end users determine the inventory levels. This just-in-time inventory philosophy works by having the upstream functions continually replace only the inventory that has been taken by the process directly downstream from it. Kanban is simply the signal used to let the upstream functions know it is time to replenish what has been taken. If you are interested in learning more about this, a Google search should give you plenty of leads.

Million-Dollar Memo:

You can't just ride the pull-through wave; you've got to plan, focus, and master the wave.

Growing Pains

Logos, advertising, packaging, demand—our name recognition was growing, and along with it was our inventory. With more inventory requirements came the need to find and rent some space in a local warehouse.

To gain market feedback from pickup truck owners, we set up a booth at a NASCAR Truck Series race at the Mansfield, Ohio, track. The feedback was very positive and useful. Once again, we were certain we were on to something.

Jim and I had set a goal to get ShurTrax offered in at least one hundred stores for the coming winter of 2004. We counted Internet, catalog, or brick and mortar stores. We accomplished it!

A national chain of farm-supply stores had open buying days where you could travel to their headquarters and show a buyer your product. We submitted, got an invite, and then succeeded in getting a twenty-store test with this great chain.

Jim and I went from sky-high to disappointment when the test proved unsuccessful. We learned that to get a test with a large chain is the easy part. Large chains test new products all the time, and very, very, *very* few succeed. Actually, I don't know how any succeed given the lack of support your product receives. The stores usually will not advertise the new product since it is only available in a small region.

We actually plugged this national chain on our *Trucks!* marketplace twenty-second commercial as "available at ..." Not only did it *not* produce, but it backfired in a big way.

The next day, the buyer called me to say, "Whatever you guys are doing, stop it. People are walking into our stores asking for your products where we don't have them, and our store personnel know nothing about them."

I couldn't believe it. We're plugging *your* store on *our* dime using cable TV, and you want us to stop? Because selling our product is harder on your employees? And this is a test that's supposed to *succeed*?

To help end the confusion, Jim and I personally visited all twenty of the test stores in an effort to train the employees on the advantages of our product. When we arrived, the story was almost the same at every location. We had to go to the back room to find our display, bring it out onto the floor, and let the manager know what it was.

I even got a call from a (stocked) store later saying that they had just sent a customer away because they did not have ShurTrax products. I told them, "I know the display is there because I personally put it up." They then found it.

I use this national chain in this example, but it was this way at several other mid- and large-size retail chains where we were given a "test."

From cable TV, we went on to networking with those in our field. As a result, we joined two influential organizations we hoped would help us better reach those who might benefit from our product: SEMA and LTAA.

SEMA stands for Specialty Equipment Market Association. LTAA stands for Light Truck Accessory Alliance and is positioned under the SEMA umbrella. Joining these associations was critical because it gave us a place to meet others in our industry and exhibit our products to potential customers. The associations paid off almost immediately. At one SEMA show we met and hired independent sales reps—and even found our first warehouse distributor, Meyer Distributing, located in Jasper, Indiana. A warehouse distributor's role is to sell your product directly to all of the independently owned retail stores, such as Pickups Plus. There are literally thousands of these types of retail stores that buy from warehouse distributors. Meyer is a great, growing company and we were ecstatic they decided to pick up the ShurTrax product line.

The largest warehouse distributor is Keystone Automotive, and we knew we were years away from getting their attention. Until then, Meyer would be a great warehouse distributor for us.

Remember, it's okay to start small as long as you *start something*!

Million-Dollar Memo:

Logos, advertising, packaging, demand—our name recognition was growing, and along with it was our inventory.

Chairman of the Board

Organization is a big part of pull-through; it's key to mastering the wave instead of sitting back and letting the wave take you where it wants to go. And speaking of "riding the wave," someone had to be "chairman of the board." One of our first organizational processes was to form a board of directors.

Ours had seven members, including Jim and I along with two local Series A lead investors, Al Bell and Bill Tanner. Jim and I along with the original family and friends investors received common stock. The Series A is the preferred stock in that it gets paid back first and therefore is less risky. We then added a representative from each angel fund: Ron Scharer from OTAF, Rich Seal from QCA, and Thomas Young from Core Network.

Next we grew out of our garage and into a more formal and professional working, storage, and supply space. With working capital and inventory on its way, we found and leased 6,400 square feet of office and warehouse space in Marion, Ohio.

Not knowing exactly how much inventory to buy, we purchased twenty thousand units based on our original forecast from a manufacturer in China. Forecasting without a sales history is pretty tricky. Although I previously explained the Kanban process to you, we were unable to follow it the first year as we established relations with our foreign supplier. This caused us to tie too much of our working capital up in inventory that first winter season.

Million-Dollar Memo:

Organization is a big part of pull-through; it's key to mastering the wave instead of sitting back and letting the wave take you where it wants to go.

Made in China

Why China and not South Carolina? The owner of the South Carolina plant sold out to a new owner who abruptly called me and said they were not interested in making ShurTrax for us. He coldly said they had already loaded up a "semi-trailer full of our raw materials" and was "sending them to Ohio."

I asked him, "What am I suppose to do with this vinyl and cartons?" He said, "That's your problem, not mine!" I then had to scramble to find an agent that would find us a manufacturer in China. Fortunately, the previous owner in South Carolina introduced me to his agent, and China has been a great supplier of our products ever since.

It was all falling into place. Now we had a warehouse and storage space to fill, and even a manufacturer to fill it for us. Over time, we had grown our product into 3,500 stores. I say "over time" because it definitely didn't happen "overnight!"

A test at Fred Meyer Stores, a subsidiary of the larger Kroger family of companies, proved worthwhile, yet unsuccessful, as we missed our season's sales numbers. The test did have some decent sales, but for a test to be successful, sometimes a sell-through in the range of 85 percent must be achieved over a certain time frame, usually between sixty and ninety days. However, advertising was beginning to catch on and the people who had bought ShurTrax loved the product.

As earlier noted, we were disappointed in our yearly sales. We had to go back to our angel investors and bank to ask for more funds. This was not fun at all. Thomas Young, the board member and investor from Core Network, stepped up to lead this round of financing. This brings to mind a warning about seeing your product through rose-colored glasses. In short, there is a fine line between viewing the glass as all the way full and totally empty.

Success does not come in absolutes. Instead, success is a culmination of a long, long, *long* series of ups and downs, triumphs and failures. Our annual sales might have been disappointing, but we knew this much: we had a product that had the potential to be a huge success.

Million-Dollar Memo:

Success does not come in absolutes. Instead, success is a culmination of a long, long, long series of ups and downs, triumphs and failures.

Gush! Splat! Blast-off!
At Last, the Pipeline Begins to Flow

Once again, it was angels to the rescue. Angel funds, that is. With the needed financing behind us, we blazed a trail with more advertising and successful sales calls. We took everything we learned in Step #6 and put it all to good use.

The trick is not to throw good money after bad. Even if it's not a lot of money, a little funding used well is *much* more valuable than lots of funding used poorly.

The work was beginning to pay off! Finally—*finally*—we were landing some huge accounts. I mean huge, deal-making accounts. And the best part was that most were more than a test. The accounts that were reordering frequently included:

- Advance Auto Parts
- Canadian Tire
- Keystone Automotive (Remember them? It was supposed to take years!)
- Warren Distribution (Warehouse distributors for Toyota. ShurTrax is now offered in 1,500 Toyota dealerships as an add-on accessory when buying a new 2007 Tundra pickup)
- JEGS
- Summit Racing
- Amazon.com
- JC Whitney
- Stylin' Concepts
- G.I. Joe's

- Owens Classic
- and many, many others ...

Million-Dollar Memo:

Even if it's not a lot of money, a little funding used well is much more valuable than lots of funding used poorly.

Epilogue

✦

Your Time to Shine

It is common sense to take a method and try it. If it fails, admit it frankly and try another. But above all, try something.

—Franklin D. Roosevelt

Success!

Sweet, *sweet* success.

It was finally official: On January 9, 2007, we were finally issued our patent; official patent # 7,159,902. It was the culmination but far from the end—of one amazing, fascinating, *incredible* journey.

When I saw that official patent number I couldn't believe how far I'd come from that newbie way back in Step #1. Just over three years had passed since the official non-provisional utility patent had been filed. I'd barely known what a patent was back then, and here I was holding my very own patent number.

I realized then that America is still the great country it had set out to become so many years ago. You can still achieve the American dream. You can still create something, bring it to market, and watch your invention make the lives of other Americans easier.

All you have to do is get started.

So what's stopping you? Have you started yet? Are you half-way through, frustrated, disappointed, let down, and ready to give up? Hold on; your time to shine is at hand. All the steps you need to take are right here in this book. That's right; I have given you everything you need to get started on bringing your idea to market today.

Yes, you'll have to do some research to fill in the gaps. Sure, there will be forms to fill out, other books to buy, Web sites to visit, and pencils to sharpen. And, of course, you are free to make your own decisions along the way.

But you'll never make any decision more important than this one: just start!

Million-Dollar Memo:

You can still achieve the American dream. You can still create something, bring it to market, and watch your invention make the lives of other Americans easier.

How Do You Define Success?

The funny thing about success is that it's just as hard to stay on top as it is to get there. It all goes back to the journey; the journey that never ends. The creation of your idea is just one step of many, many steps that don't end until, well, until you do. So settle in, enjoy the journey, and don't give yourself unrealistic deadlines—or expectations.

Ask yourself, "How do I define success?" Is it just money that drives you forward? Or how many stores your product is in? Or how big the stores are? Or how colorful the packaging is? Or how popular the product is? All of these are typical ways of gauging success, but which one is right for you?

One way to keep yourself sane is to keep everything in perspective. Go back to your plan, keep managing your spreadsheets and other sources of organization, and don't let current success stop you from planning for future success.

For instance, establishing the pipeline with retailers is very difficult. The payoff is when you see them begin to reorder with more frequency. You then know the advertising is beginning to work for you, and you shift your focus from landing these accounts to supporting them.

For me, *that's* success.

Our staff has grown modestly to four full-time employees and one part-time employee.

For me, *that's* success.

As president and CEO, I have had to delegate some of my responsibilities. However, the one function I refuse to give up is reading and answering each e-mail we receive from our customers. That's right; I act as the customer service rep.

For me, *that's* success.

I don't mind; far from it. In fact, it keeps me in touch with any issues we have with our products. I plan on continuing this until we have a perfect product. I already have a few more changes in mind for next year's ShurTrax that will remove any negative issues we have had in the past. By constantly upgrading, year after year, I know we will eventually meet our goal of being known by both our retail partners and end users as the greatest manufacturer to work within our industry.

For me, *that's* success.

How about you?

Million-Dollar Memo:

The funny thing about success is that it's just as hard to stay on top as it is to get there.

The Next B.I.G. Idea

ShurTrax was just the beginning. Not wanting to have a company with only a winter-type product, I began to think of an idea that would fit our niche (truck beds) for the other three seasons.

Watching people back their pickups up to racetracks and soccer games gave me an idea to design a rigid and collapsible type of bleacher-seating arrangement that could be used to watch events from. I have named the apparatus "UpFront Seats" and the provisional and now non-provisional patents have already been filed. We conducted a focus group study and hope to soon begin work on the initial prototypes.

What makes this idea the next big idea?

Well, let's apply the B.I.G. Idea Test and see:

- **B-old:** Be bold. Think of things no one has thought of before. Take a problem and make it a solution. I could have just improvised those little padded seats they hand out at stadiums, and that would have been a good enough idea. But I'm not interested in being "good enough." Bleacher seats bring the family together; they make a simple game an event. Now that's *big*!

- **I-ngenious:** For an idea to be big you must look to the ordinary for the extraordinary. What can you do to make the day special? How can you create something out of nothing? By watching pickup trucks back into games and seeing people fool around with blankets, pillows, coolers, and all other types, sizes, and makes of uncomfortable seating, I was able to devise a solution that folded perfectly onto the success we've had with ShurTrax products.

- **G-rand:** Bleacher seats in your truck bed! Convenience, comfort, and creativity, all in one product. It's one idea on a *grand* scale, and I'm proud to be able to add it to the SealPak Innovations family of products. Remember, you have to think B.I.G.!

Million-Dollar Memo:

Be bold. Think of things no one has thought of before. Take a problem and make it a solution.

UpFront Seats

UpFront Seats will be our next product. What do you think?

What's Your Million-Dollar Idea?

The time is now; the time is yours. Start thinking now of that next B.I.G. idea. Now. Today. Not next week, or next month, or next year, or next ... anything. Stop making excuses and make it happen. You know you can; you know you want to. Otherwise, why would you still be along for the journey?

It's human nature to put off our dreams. There are the kids to think about, the mortgage to pay, and the nine to five job. All of these are plusses, not minuses. Think how proud your kids would be to walk into a store and say to their friends, "Look! My mom/dad invented that!"

Think of ways to involve your spouse and other loved ones in the process. Look how my brothers helped me out of jams along the way. Don't you think your spouse, family, and even friends would want to do the same for you?

And your job? That can be a valuable resource, too. Don't think of it as a job; think of it as funding. Don't think of your coworkers as colleagues; think of them as potential investors, engineers, manufacturers, or even customers.

It's not aptitude that prevents us from achieving our dreams; it's attitude. If I had ever stopped to consider myself a failure at any point along my own personal, incredible journey through the invention process, I would have been done for, sunk, doomed.

If I've taught you anything in this book, it's to believe in yourself. Look what I achieved, with very little "know how" about the process—until I lived it for myself. I've done the hard part; I've made the mistakes so you won't have to. Now all you have to do is learn from them and achieve your dreams just that much quicker.

It all boils down to the idea. If you believe in your idea strongly enough, passionately enough, others will too. So many people helped me along the way to that official patent number, and as much as I like myself I know it wasn't because of me so much as it was the idea.

With all of that being said, I hope I haven't made this sound as if I have "got it made" with the ShurTrax products. If you want to hear a rags to riches ending, I may have to write another book someday, because this story doesn't end that way. Even though we have come a long way, there are still plenty of uncertainties in this story. We are currently contemplating selling the ShurTrax product line due to more financial needs than we may be able to overcome. If it is time to sell, then I am prepared to do that. If you remember, that was part of the deal when we accepted our angel investors' money. At this point in my journey those issues are secondary. The main thing is I had an idea and I didn't just let it lay there. I put together a great team of people over a four year span that have accomplished the feat of selling more than one million-dollars worth of ShurTrax to grateful customers.

I sincerely hope you get to take this invention journey for yourself and I would be thrilled to think this book helped you along your way.

So, now it's time to ask yourself: What's *your* million-dollar idea?

And one more question: How soon can you begin to patent it?

Million-Dollar Memo:

Start thinking now of that next B.I.G. idea. Stop making excuses and make it happen.

978-0-595-44474-8
0-595-44474-1

Printed in the United States
94657LV00002B/19/A

9 780595 444748